A Special Gift

Presented to:

Sharon — my dear soul-mate
Happy Birthday

From:

Emily

Date:

03/01/01

Sayings, Scriptures, and Stories from
the Bible Revealing God's Love

hugs
from
Heaven™

Portraits
of a
Woman's
Faith

Deb Cleveland

HOWARD
PUBLISHING CO.

Our purpose at Howard Publishing is to:

- *Increase faith* in the hearts of growing Christians
- *Inspire holiness* in the lives of believers
- *Instill hope* in the hearts of struggling people everywhere

Because He's coming again!

Hugs from Heaven—Portraits of a Woman's Faith
© 2000 by Deb Cleveland
All rights reserved. Printed in the United States of America

Published by Howard Publishing Co., Inc.,
3117 North 7th Street, West Monroe, LA 71291-2227

00 01 02 03 04 05 06 07 08 09   10 9 8 7 6 5 4 3 2 1

Paraphrased Scriptures by LeAnn Weiss, owner of Encouragement Company,
3006 Brandywine Dr., Orlando, FL 32806

Edited by Philis Boultinghouse
Interior design by Stephanie Denney
Photography by LinDee Loveland

Library of Congress Cataloging-in-Publication Data
Cleveland, Deb, 1951–
   Hugs from heaven : portraits of a woman's faith : sayings, scriptures, and stories from
the Bible revealing God's love / Deb Cleveland ; personalized scriptures by LeAnn Weiss.
   p. cm.
  ISBN 1-58229-129-2
   1. Christian women—Prayer-books and devotions—English. 2. Women in the Bible—
Meditations. I. Title.

BV4844.C59 2000
242'.643—dc21

                                                00-040858

Contents

Introduction vii

1. Daughter of Destiny 1

2. Daughter of Devotion 17

3. Daughter of Forgiveness 33

4. Daughter of Confidence 49

5. Daughter of Boldness 69

6. Daughter of Determination . 85

7. Daughter of Trust 101

Introduction

The *Hugs from Heaven* series is written with one purpose in mind: to make God's love more real and refreshing. This book is divided into topical sections consisting of a paraphrased scripture, an inspirational message, a poignant saying, a fictional story based on a particular passage of Scripture, and the actual account of the story from Scripture. Even though the narrative is fictional and the writer takes a creative course with the story, the biblical truths are uncompromised. Favorite Bible stories take on new meaning as you are transported to the scene to explore the thoughts and feelings of women of faith who were touched by Jesus' embrace in a special way. May the message in this book and all the *Hugs from Heaven* books bring honor to God and praise to our Savior, Jesus Christ.

God is the God of human history, and

He is at work continuously, mysteriously,

accomplishing His eternal purposes in us,

through us, for us, and in spite of us.

—ELISABETH ELLIOT

Chapter 1

Daughter of Destiny

My Precious Daughter, I've blessed you with My indescribable gift of Jesus. I know the plans I have for you. My plans for you are the best, offering you a hope-filled future. Even before you were born, I purposely ordained all of your days. As you trust in Me, I'll fill you with all joy and peace. Allow Me to flood your life with hope by the power of My Holy Spirit.

Love,

Your God of All Hope

—from 2 Corinthians 9:15; Jeremiah 29:11; Psalm 139:16; Romans 15:13

Have you ever been called by God to do something really hard? Like forgiving someone when you didn't want to? Loving someone you didn't like? Smiling when you'd rather stick out your tongue?

You see, being chosen by God usually means that tough stuff is ahead. It usually means you're going to have to take a few hits, endure some pain, and get your hands dirty. Being favored by God means you'll eventually have to follow Him to the river, through the valley, across the desert, and finally to the hill. In other words, being favored by God is a privilege that will most likely break your heart.

On the other hand, being favored by God should bring you to your knees in thanksgiving and have you skipping along the rooftops with joy and dancing in the streets with the most delicious abandonment.

Yeah, you'll be tired, dirty, sweaty, and achy, but when you sit down at night, your heart will be bursting to sing. It will be dipped in a sweetness that is only possible when one has walked directly behind Jesus—footprint for footprint.

Being called means you'll love a betrayer, forgive an

adulteress, feed the hungry, clothe the poor, and probably have only one pair of sandals. But it also means that at the end of the day you'll eat a hot dinner prepared by Christ Himself. And if need be, He'll even spoon-feed you and wipe your chin.

God only calls the great ones. Great by His standards—not yours. He's partial to grandmothers, mothers, daughters, cousins, aunts, housewives, widows, seamstresses, queens, slave girls, and shepherds' wives.

A pliable heart and willing spirit seem to be the only qualifications. Even then, God has a way of softening the hardest of hearts and coaxing the most stubborn spirit to His way of thinking.

Being favored by God will hurt. But in the end, heaven's gate will open when it sees you approach, angels will applaud your entry, and God will call you by name.

Hang in there; the best is yet to be.

If you have God, you have a future—

and it's not a dismal one.

—KAY ARTHUR

Hope Is Born

"Hold me up; hold me up!" urged Mary.

Joseph rushed to his wife's side and did as he was told. What he feared most had happened. This baby was going to be born without the aid of a midwife or his mother-in-law. A prayer was never far from his lips.

Mary held her breath and waited for the pain to subside. The straw-filled stable floor beneath her was becoming more than she could bear. It itched. It was hot. It was sticking to her. The child within her would wait no longer. Mary had felt the pangs of labor all day during their journey. At times, riding upon the small donkey was excruciating, and she chose to walk. When walking was no longer possible, with Joseph's help, she returned to the moist swayback of the animal and once again endured the jostling ride.

Mary longed for the comforting touch of her mother but knew that this way was best. The census gave them an excuse to leave home. The timing couldn't have been better. Except for her cousin, Elizabeth, no one knew of the secret of this child's miraculous conception. Its incredibility and unbelievability caused Mary to wonder constantly about what kind of birth to expect. Because of her uncertainty, she wanted no one from her family to witness it. Would the angel Gabriel attend? Would God Himself show His face and catch the child in His own arms? Would the sky burst open when the baby drew His first breath? What would the Son of God look like?

For months, Mary pondered all these thoughts in her heart. And Joseph? *What must he be thinking right now?* thought Mary. Moving about her, Joseph could not have been more attentive or loving. Yet his shaking hands told her that he, too, was bewildered by it all. He would frequently touch her hand or arm, expressing his tender concern. He constantly rearranged the straw about her in whatever way she requested. *I must be making him crazy,* she thought. During the pains, at times she called for him to comfort her, and then the next minute, she'd be irritated and order him not to touch her.

The salt, extra cloth, and little water pot she brought with her were lying close at hand.

"Now, Joseph, when the baby comes, you must wipe Him down with the salt and wrap Him quickly in the cloth," Mary instructed through gritted teeth. The pain was now constant.

"I cut the cord first, though, right?" asked the nervous husband.

Mary just looked at him and rolled her eyes. How many times had they gone over this in the last hour?

A few minutes later, Joseph leaned over Mary and gently touched his forehead to hers, and for a brief second they were able to shut it all out. It was just the two of them—Mary and Joseph. But the pain did not allow them much time for intimacy, as it grew fierce and demanding.

Mary concentrated on the task at hand. She focused her

gaze upon the doorway of the stable. From where she lay, she could see just beyond the opening. Slivers of dark sky dotted with thousands of stars danced through the entrance. She squeezed Joseph's hand to give them both courage. How many hours had they lain awake at night sharing their thoughts—preparing themselves for this very moment? But Mary now knew that nothing could prepare anyone for this moment.

The actual birth came swiftly. Before Mary and Joseph knew it, they were staring into the tiny face of a squirming God. Lying on His mother's belly, the infant found His thumb while trying to focus His eyes upon His mother. Joseph began the ritual of wiping the infant down with salt and cautiously swaddling Him in the clean cloth.

Many of Mary's questions were answered at once—He was just a baby, no bright flashes of Gabriel, and yes, she could not deny the presence of God all about her. She knew that if she could but scratch the air only slightly, God would be visible just on the other side.

The new mother glanced between her newborn and her speechless husband. How quickly love expanded to include a child. The three of them bonded instantly and irreversibly became a family. That was just as much a miracle as the conception, thought Mary.

Tears began streaming down her cheeks, spilling upon the infant's round head. Mary lay back on her bed of hay while cradling her son in her arms. Joseph wrapped them both in a blanket and stepped outside into the night air in relief.

Mary looked into the scrunched face of her baby. His cheeks were as soft as the moss on the banks of a stream. His fingers smelled like new grass in spring. God had indeed favored her with sweetness. Yet Mary dared not fool herself— the price of favor was also usually bought with sorrow. But she would not think of that now. She was tired. The infant was drifting to sleep. The mother pulled her son near to her face and whispered, "While You are in my care, You will be safe, my love. My soul exalts You, and my spirit has rejoiced in God, my Savior. My little one, I will give You the best part of me forever. Whatever You call me to do, I will do. Wherever You call me to go, I will go. "

Sleep came swiftly to mother and child.

While the heavens danced, twirled, and cheered, God

Daughter of Destiny

smiled. Hope was born on this day, and the God of all creation proclaimed it good—very, very good.

In those days Caesar Augustus issued a decree that a census should be taken of the entire Roman world. (This was the first census that took place while Quirinius was governor of Syria.) And everyone went to his own town to register.

So Joseph also went up from the town of Nazareth in Galilee to Judea, to Bethlehem the town of David, because he belonged to the house and line of David. He went there to register with Mary, who was pledged to be married to him and was expecting a child. While they were there, the time came for the baby to be born, and she gave birth to her firstborn, a son. She wrapped him in cloths and placed him in a manger, because there was no room for them in the inn.

—Luke 2:1–7

Reflections on times when God inspired new hope in me…

_____

_____

_____

_____

_____

_____

_____

_____

_____

_____

_____

_____

_____

_____

*For the LORD God is a sun and shield; the LORD bestows favor
and honor; no good thing does he withhold
from those whose walk is blameless. —Psalm 84:11*

May the favor of the Lord our God rest upon us;
establish the work of our hands for us—yes, establish
the work of our hands. —Psalm 90:17

_____

_____

_____

_____

_____

_____

_____

_____

_____

_____

_____

_____

_____

"For I know the plans I have for you," declares the LORD,
"plans to prosper you and not to harm you,
plans to give you hope and a future." —Jeremiah 29:11

Chapter 2

Daughter of Devotion

I've designed you to walk by faith, not by sight. Receive what I've promised through faith and patience. I'm devoted to completing the good work I've started in you. Even when you're old and gray, I'll sustain you. May you hold firmly to the hope that you've confessed, knowing that you can absolutely trust Me to follow through. When you love Me and obey My commands, I keep My agreement of love for a thousand lifetimes.

Faithfully,

Your Promise Keeper

—from 2 Corinthians 5:7; Hebrews 6:12; Philippians 1:6; Isaiah 46:4; Hebrews 10:23; Deuteronomy 7:9

Have you ever felt useless? Have you ever felt that time has passed you by and that your life has accounted for nothing?

Well, think again. God expects great things from His women—*all* of His women.

Time does not diminish your value—not to God.

Age does not determine your worth—not to God.

If anything, as we age, we become dearer, not drearier—at least to God.

Look in the mirror. God made that face—as it is today. The lines that appear, He has gently kissed into place.

Now place your hand over your heart. Feel it beating? Until it stops, God expects something from you.

Know what it is?

Faithfulness.

When you doubt His love, you are to remember His cross.

When you waver from fear, you are to reclaim His boldness.

When you flinch at Satan's stare, you are to direct your eyes upward.

When you become weary, you are to reach out your hand for His.

When the world says, "No," you are to remind them of Jesus' "Yes!"

You are worthy. You were made with great care. The passing of time only makes you more precious. The mountains were made in your honor. The gardenia's sweet smell reminds God of you. And under His fingernails you still linger.

Remain faithful...and God will do the rest.

God's definition of beauty is a lot different than the world's. God says that beauty is found in a gentle, quiet, and obedient spirit.

—*HEATHER WHITESTONE*

Faithfulness Rewarded

The Jerusalem landscape glistened as the trees grabbed the sunrise, painting themselves a shimmering gold. The city was awakening to a new day, and Anna, the old prophetess, greeted it as she had greeted every morning for more than fifty years—on bent knee by her upstairs temple chamber window. She believed this to be the most sacred moment of the day. She could almost see the actual hand of God pat the head of the moon "good night" and embrace the shoulders of the sun "good morning."

Anna gave the streets of Jerusalem one more glance and was about to pull herself up from the stone floor when she saw them. Just entering the city—the man, carrying a small cage holding two turtledoves; the woman, sitting gracefully upon her miniature steed; and the child—held closely to His mother's breast.

The donkey carrying mother and infant didn't seem to mind his passengers. He walked as if the path under his hooves were the softest pasture instead of the hardened dust that it was. But it was the child who caused Anna's heart to leap. "The Redeemer comes!" she said out loud.

At age eighty-four, Anna's heart was still as pliable as a young believer's. Each day brought new discovery, and with each breath, she inhaled hope. And now, hope was coming to her on the back of a donkey.

As she left her temple chamber to greet the approaching family, her mind whirled through the years. Every stone that gave the temple its stature, every pillar on which she had leaned, and every altar that cushioned her knees were now old friends. How full her life had been. Now, blessing upon blessing, she would greet God Himself sitting upon His mother's lap.

Faithfulness Rewarded

As she entered the courtyard, she marveled at the earthly parents of the Messiah. How ordinary they looked. How humble was their carriage. They were chosen to nurture the Prince of Peace, but nothing about them spoke of privilege—no jewels bespeckled their cloaks, no purple trim heralded their holy calling. Simple was their look, yet the sun streaking through the temple court seemed deliberate in its aim as it created a bright halo all around them.

When Anna arrived, she saw her dear friend Simeon excitedly watching the young family enter the court. At the sight of this aging, righteous man, tears swelled in Anna's eyes. She knew God had promised Simeon long ago that he would live long enough to see the Savior. And today that promise would be fulfilled.

Mary and Joseph waited for their cue from those ordained. Mary must be purified for giving birth, and their infant son must be consecrated.

God's Spirit nudged Simeon toward the couple. The time had come. The Messiah had arrived! Simeon now cradled God. God would soon cradle Simeon.

Anna took her place on the temple steps. When she did, God smiled at this flower that had bloomed in the desert. While Satan had tried countless times to plant dark seeds within her, she had not allowed it. Bitterness could not find fertile ground in her heart. How strongly she believed. How loyal she had been—a servant from her knees to her heart. How God cherished her faithfulness.

As an army of one, this powerful woman had personified all God had intended women and men to be: strong, pure, compassionate, committed, nurturing, and in love—with life, with creation, and with Him.

God could not remember a day since Anna's youth when she did not call upon His name, praise His power, and give thanks for His generosity. In the dismal hours after the death of her husband, when others would have cursed Him, Anna begged Him to use her as a vessel of goodness.

And now, God's eyes did not leave Anna as she peered into the face of His infant Son. She was not fooled by His miniature countenance or toothless grin. She was not surprised that the King came in swaddling clothes. She was not confused that the fate of the world was in His small, curled fist. Anna's faithfulness was rewarded with confidence. She recognized God, the infant, immediately because she knew God, the Father, so well.

The rituals were performed. Joseph, Mary, and Jesus went safely back home. Simeon laid his head down on his pillow for the last time. And, Anna, lovely Anna, slept in her temple chamber. She was tired, and her body gave way to the fatigue that old bones feel. Yet her heart had a stronger beat than yesterday. For today, she had kissed the tiny knuckles of God Himself!

The next morning Anna once again found herself on bent knee greeting the day with prayer. Nothing had changed, yet everything had changed. The Redeemer had finally come, and Anna knew there was much to do. Slowly she rose from the stone floor, gazed one last time at the rising sun, and then turned to go do it. So beats the heart of a faithful servant.

God so loved...that He gave His only Son....

Scriptural Account

When the time of their purification according to the Law of Moses had been completed, Joseph and Mary took him to

Daughter of Devotion

Jerusalem to present him to the Lord (as it is written in the Law of the Lord, "Every firstborn male is to be consecrated to the Lord"), and to offer a sacrifice in keeping with what is said in the Law of the Lord: "a pair of doves or two young pigeons."

Now there was a man in Jerusalem called Simeon, who was righteous and devout. He was waiting for the consolation of Israel, and the Holy Spirit was upon him. It had been revealed to him by the Holy Spirit that he would not die before he had seen the Lord's Christ. Moved by the Spirit, he went into the temple courts. When the parents brought in the child Jesus to do for him what the custom of the Law required, Simeon took him in his arms and praised God, saying:

"Sovereign Lord, as you have promised,
  you now dismiss your servant in peace.
For my eyes have seen your salvation,
  which you have prepared in the sight of all
   people,
a light for revelation to the Gentiles
  and for glory to your people Israel."

The child's father and mother marveled at what was said about him. Then Simeon blessed them and said to Mary, his mother: "This child is destined to cause the falling and rising of many in Israel, and to be a sign that will be spoken against, so that the thoughts of many hearts will be revealed. And a sword will pierce your own soul too."

There was also a prophetess, Anna, the daughter of Phanuel, of the tribe of Asher. She was very old; she had lived with her husband seven years after her marriage, and then was a widow until she was eighty-four. She never left the temple but worshiped night and day, fasting and praying. Coming up to them at that very moment, she gave thanks to God and spoke about the child to all who were looking forward to the redemption of Jerusalem.

When Joseph and Mary had done everything required by the Law of the Lord, they returned to Galilee to their own town of Nazareth.

—Luke 2:22–39

Reflections on God's faithfulness in my life...

_____

_____

_____

_____

_____

_____

_____

_____

_____

_____

_____

_____

For the LORD loves the just
and will not forsake his faithful ones.
—Psalm 37:28

Be joyful in hope,
patient in affliction, faithful in prayer.
— Romans 12:12

Chapter 3

Daughter of
Forgiveness

You've been chosen. Don't follow the ways of the world. Instead, choose My best for you and learn what is good and pleasing to Me. I've called you out of darkness into My marvelous light. As far as the east is from the west, I've removed your sins from you. Forget your past, straining toward the future. Go for the goal, and obtain the prize for which I've called you.

Cleansing you whiter than snow,

Your Savior

P. S. Remember, forgiveness is essential. If you don't forgive others, I won't forgive you.

—from 1 Peter 2:9; Romans 12:2; Psalm 103:12; Philippians 3:13–14; Matthew 6:14–15

Choices. Life is made up of them.
Cheat or not cheat.
Curse or not curse.
Help or not help.
Wound or not wound.

Chances are you haven't always made the right choices. In fact, you may have even made some big blunders—mistakes, devastating mistakes—the kind that hurt, destroy, and leave smoldering ruins.

It hurts to acknowledge that, doesn't it? Shame pulls a crimson blush across your face like a heavy curtain. It splatters your heart on the floor of your soul like a dropped sandbag. You had a choice—and you chose poorly.

So what do you do now?

Run? Hide? Nothing?

You make another choice, of course. This time you choose better. You humble yourself and ask to be forgiven. You walk up to the door. Knock. And then scoop up your shattered heart and hand it over to God.

He'll forgive you, and then He'll heal you—because He's the only one who can. Your creation made you His

business. The cross gave Him that right. He makes you new again because He wills it.

Just ask. And when you do, no power on this earth, above or below, will keep Him from you.

You are that special. You are that forgiven.

Your eyes see your guilt.

Your faith sees his blood.

—*MAX LUCADO*

Only God

As they dragged her through the cobbled streets, she was in a daze. Only moments before, an angry mob of men had burst into her home and snatched her from her bed and her lover's arms. They roughly wrapped the bed linen around her and pulled her from the darkened room through the open door out into the bright light of day. As callused hands pulled her away from her home, she caught glimpses of the veiled eyes of her neighbors. She had betrayed them all. Loneliness was no excuse—at least not in the light of day— not where eyes could see and reflect on her actions.

Heads quickly turned. Mothers scurried children away

from her. She was now a plague—something to be purged from among them. Her life was over. If the shame did not kill her on this little parade through town, the jagged stones soon hurled at her would.

She searched for her lover. But to her surprise, she was the single attraction. The parade began and ended with her. She became more confused—enraged and horrified all at once. Her utterances to God clogged in her throat. As an adulteress and a woman, she had no right to call His name. His wrath was all she deserved. How sorry she was. How disappointed God must be. Now it was too late.

Where was she? She had lost track of her path. They were driving her as if she were a mangy calf.

Ah...the temple court.

She had never been this far inside this holy place before. Women were allowed to sit only in the shadows, veiled, barely seen, never heard. She felt this crazy urge to laugh. She was certainly being seen now! What a magnificent place. How different it looked when not viewed through encumbered eyes.

The sinful woman was thrown at the feet of Jesus—a man

she had never seen before. Who He was didn't matter to her. He was her judge, her executioner. His name was unimportant. Yet she couldn't help but look into His face, even though she knew the Law forbade it.

The moment she saw Jesus' face, fear left her. Nearly naked, moments from death; yet all of a sudden, she was not afraid. "God, forgive me of this fearlessness," she muttered. She should be frightened, not breathing, already dead. But this man's face was like no other—ordinary, but not; dark, yet full of light; grave, yet hopeful. He had not been one of her lovers, yet there was an instant intimacy between them.

The crowd became silent in waves. Those closest to Jesus hushed the others behind them. The bravest of the woman's accusers began her trial: "This woman is an adulteress, caught in the very act. The Law says she must die." And then facing Jesus, he asked, "What do You say?"

Jesus looked at the woman. What she saw in His eyes revived her fatigued legs. As she gathered her covers about her, she slowly made her way to her feet. Every part of her ached, yet she refused to be sentenced while sprawled in the dirt like tossed-out cabbage.

Jesus smiled.

Then the peculiar happened.

He knelt down and began writing in the sand. As He wrote, the crowd pushed toward Him, trying to look at what He was scribbling. For the woman, time stopped. She heard the distant clanging of a bell, and a bird fluttered among the temple pillars above her. But she dared not take her eyes off this man who held her destiny in His hands. His back looked strong, His fingers stout as they pushed their way through the sand in fluent motion—as if He were taking dictation. The words He wrote formed around her, circling her. "Who is He?" her heart yearned to know.

Those closest in the circle began backing away from Him, as the words in the sand sucked the venom from them. They began muttering under their hearts, some saying, "He must be from God," others, "He must be from Satan."

Jesus was asked again, but with much less insistence, what to do with her.

He stood and looked the whole crowd in the eye. "Kill her if you must, but only the ones without sin cast the stones." He then quietly stooped and continued with His

writing. To the woman, the words He wrote began to feel like a fortress around her.

Time was playing tricks on her now. One by one, the angry mob that had been all too eager to put her to death simply left. Some laid the stones they had planned to crush her with at her feet. Others dropped them where they stood. Others retreated with them still clinched in their fists. None would look her in the eye. The retreat seemed to the woman to take hours. She clutched her flimsy sheet so tightly around herself that her fingers had lost all feeling. Her back, once strong and straight, now felt like an old crumbling stone wall on the verge of ruin.

When all were gone, Jesus finally stood up next to her— only inches away. His closeness made her feel cloaked in purple richness instead of the tattered bed linens she actually wore. "Did no one condemn you?" He asked.

"No, Lord, no one." The sound of her own voice seemed to come from a distant tunnel.

"Then neither do I. Go. Live your life as I had meant it."

The woman could not move. Her head told her to turn, run, flee like a lamb granted reprieve from slaughter. But her heart would not let her budge. She wanted to kiss Him, cling to His feet, thank Him in some worthy way. But instead she was rooted in the sand. His scribbling surrounded her. How she wished she could read the words that halted the crowd. The ground they were imprinted on was holy; she was sure of that. This man was not man. He had given her life back to her. No, that wasn't true. He had given her *new* life. Only God had that right. Only God had that power. *Only God.*

She backed away from Him slowly, wanting to look at Him for as long as possible. She had encountered God, and He had made her matter. She would no longer be veiled to the life she was meant to live.

The everyday temple activities resumed. The footprints of those walking about began scattering the words in the sand. As the words disappeared, she felt her heart become purer. "Only God," she whispered through her tears, *"Only God."*

Scriptural Account

But Jesus went to the Mount of Olives. At dawn he appeared again in the temple courts, where all the people gathered around him, and he sat down to teach them. The teachers of the law and the Pharisees brought in a woman caught in adultery. They made her stand before the group and said to Jesus, "Teacher, this woman was caught in the act of adultery. In the Law Moses commanded us to stone such women. Now what do you say?" They were using this question as a trap, in order to have a basis for accusing him.

But Jesus bent down and started to write on the ground with his finger. When they kept on questioning him, he straightened up and said to them, "If any one of you is without sin, let him be the first to throw a stone at her." Again he stooped down and wrote on the ground.

At this, those who heard began to go away one at a time, the older ones first, until only Jesus was left, with the woman still standing there. Jesus straightened up and asked her, "Woman, where are they? Has no one condemned you?"

"No one, sir," she said.

"Then neither do I condemn you," Jesus declared. "Go now and leave your life of sin."

—John 8:1–11

Reflections on God's forgiveness in my life...

_____

_____

_____

_____

_____

_____

_____

_____

_____

_____

_____

_____

*Be kind and compassionate to one another,
forgiving each other, just as in Christ God forgave you.
—Ephesians 4:32*

Blessed are they whose transgressions are forgiven,
whose sins are covered.
—Romans 4:7

Chapter 4

Daughter of Confidence

Be confident that you will experience My goodness in the land of the living. You don't have to be afraid, because I'm your helper. Approach My throne of grace with confidence to receive mercy and all-sufficient grace in your time of need. Remember, in all things you are more than a victorious overcomer because I love you. Be convinced that nothing, not even death, can separate you from My unconditional love for you. You are blessed and fruitful when you place your confidence in Me alone.

Love,
Your God of Comfort

—from Psalm 27:13; Hebrews 13:6; 4:16;
Romans 8:37–39; Jeremiah 17:7–8

The trick is to believe even when it seems there's nothing there, to love when you don't have that loving feeling, and to stay focused when the world becomes a whirligig—moving too fast and blurring all the colors.

As a woman of the new millennium, how do you do that? How do you distinguish good from best? How do you spend your time, money, and energy in a world that thinks of you as its property—just another cog in the wheel?

The answer? You possess and guard a heart that gives Satan absolutely no hope! *You possess and guard a heart that gives Satan absolutely no hope!* When you lose focus (and you will), you leave the kitchen, the work room, the office, and the nursery. You get on your knees, and you get it back!

You remember that the seas were filled up by the hand of God—the same hand that escorted you onto this earth.

You remember that the tomb is empty—emptied by the same power that gave yesterday its sunrise.

You remember that you are never, ever alone—no matter how dark, bright, quiet, or noisy your days become.

You wipe your hands on your apron, you leave your keyboard silent, and you turn the oven off—just long enough to remember the one true thing:

God is great. God is good. God is here—now and forever.

Trouble is one of God's great servants

because it reminds us how much we

continually need the Lord.

—JIM CYMBALA

The One True Thing

The stress and pain of recent days had left Martha like a soggy rag, floating atop the Jordan. Her brother, Lazarus, lay dead in the family tomb. Her sister, Mary, was surrounded by mourners in the front room.

Finally left to herself, Martha paced around her open stove. She dipped her fingers in the small jar of water she carried and sprinkled drops upon the heating stones of the hearth. The stones sizzled, indicating they were ready for the dough to be spread upon them. Martha looked around the small room at the several loaves of bread already prepared, brought in by neighbors and friends. Each loaf was wrapped in cloth and was waiting to be served when needed. Making more bread made no sense. But then, nothing made sense to Martha now. Lazarus was dead, and Jesus hadn't come.

Martha found it hard to concentrate as she scooped the dough from the clay platter she had formed it in. The feel of the soft batter in her hands usually gave her comfort. But now the dough stuck between her fingers just like the sadness stuck to her heart.

"Why did He not come?" she said aloud. "Why?" Martha leaned against the brick wall to keep from crumpling to the floor. She pressed a towel over her mouth so those in the front room could not hear the deep moan swelling within her. Tears dripped down her cheeks and along her neck, dampening the top of her dress.

After a few moments, Martha numbly went back to her dough and began to spread it upon the heated stones. As she did, her thoughts went to Jesus. She had loved and believed in Him from the very first moment she saw Him. How long ago was that now?

She smiled as she remembered that first encounter. She

had invited Him and His followers into her home for a meal. But it wasn't long before she'd found the preparations to feed so many on such short notice overwhelming. When she realized that Mary was not helping her at all but staying in the other room with Jesus, she asked her special guest to send her sister into the kitchen to help. Mary was always getting distracted.

Martha got help that day, but not in the way she'd expected. "Martha, Martha, so many things worry and bother you, but really only *one* truly matters. And Mary has chosen that one," said Jesus.

Even in reprimand, He was tender. Martha had learned a great lesson that day and had tried hard not to repeat her foolishness, although it was a battle not to get caught up in the busyness of the hour. Many times since then, she, too, sat at Jesus' feet and listened to His tremendous stories. She had lost count of the many loaves of bread she had burnt on His behalf.

When Jesus spoke, Martha was sure she heard the voice of God. That voice was eternal and had sung in places she could only imagine.

Daughter of Confidence

Martha sighed heavily. "Why wasn't He here?"

Suddenly someone in the front room shouted, "Jesus is coming!"

Martha immediately dropped her towel, left her bread, and ran to meet Him. Her mind flooded with words she wanted to say, but when she reached Him, her heart spoke first. "Had you been here, my brother would not be dead," she cried. Martha fell at Jesus' feet and looked up into His face. She felt sure that if He had been here, He would have saved her brother—healed him, cleansed him inside and out. Suddenly Martha's soul calmed and the realization of Jesus' power became clear. She reached for His hands and pleaded, "But even now I know that whatever You ask of God, God will give You."

Jesus pulled Martha to Him and let her words soothe His sadness—for they were not condemnations of blame but proclamations of faith! She knew His power. She understood it.

Jesus answered, "Your brother will rise again."

She looked up at Him and said, "I know, Master. You have taught me about the resurrection of the last days."

The One True Thing

Jesus whispered in her ear, "Martha, I *am* the resurrection and the life; he who believes in Me shall live, even if he dies, and everyone who lives and believes in Me shall never die. Do you believe this?"

Martha looked into the face of Jesus. It was as familiar to her as her own. The strength of its image was imprinted on her soul. Her eyes did not flicker. Her mind did not waver. "Yes, Lord. I believe you are the Christ, the Son of God, the Messiah, the Coming One."

Martha's confession thundered through Jesus like a mighty wind. Her faith wrapped His lamenting spirit in a strong embrace.

Martha then left to get Mary and tell her the news of Jesus' arrival. When she heard, Mary came running and greeted Jesus with the very same words Martha had uttered earlier, "Lord, if you had been here, my brother would not have died."

As Jesus witnessed the pain and distress of those He loved, He was deeply moved, and He wept. The three of them embraced like family. Their arms intertwined, their heads touching, their small circle impenetrable.

Finally, Jesus could wait no longer. Death had had enough playtime. With the sisters at His side, Jesus led them to Lazarus's tomb. Martha's heart pounded in her ears as if thousands of angels were crowding in around them, fluttering their massive wings in unison.

As Jesus called for the entry stone to be rolled away, the wrestling of Martha's spirit between faith and fear caused her to cry out, "But the stench!"

Jesus looked down at His most practical Martha. He remembered her as an infant in her mother's womb. Had she been able, He was sure she would have been born with a broom and apron attached and her hands on her hip.

"Martha, did I not say to you, if you believe you will see the glory of God?"

Once again, a gentle reprimand.

When the stone was rolled away, Jesus cried out with a loud voice, "Lazarus, come forth!" The ancient voice caused Martha to fall to her knees. The tenderness of it reprimanded with love. The boldness of it called back the dead. In the beginning that voice had called the world to become and behave, and now, booming by her side, it called her own tiny world to order.

Those crowding around became as statues. All hearts stopped in midbeat. The air around them suddenly grew plump with the sweet fragrance of roses and lilacs. Birds folded their wings and perched themselves together by the hundreds on twigs, boulders, and shrubs. The wind lost its breath. The clouds hovered motionless. And then from inside the tomb came a faint sound. Those outside strained to hear and took a step closer. The sound grew stronger and louder until it could no longer be mistaken—it was the laughter of Lazarus!

Emerging from the cave, wrapped in cloth from head to toe, struggling to walk, came Lazarus, and he was laughing— loudly, boldly, triumphantly, as if life were made only for joy!

Jesus commanded that His friend be unbound and set free. As the crowd scurried to obey, Jesus looked down upon Martha, who was still kneeling. Her legs would not hold her, her hands were clasped lightly on her lap, and her tears flowed as a stream, fresh and cleansing. The look on Martha's face told Jesus that faith had won and that Martha was not surprised to see her brother emerge from the dark tomb. In fact, her heart had expected it all along.

Jesus smiled. Never had He loved her more. "Martha, Martha," He said, "my beloved Martha."

Scriptural Account

On his arrival, Jesus found that Lazarus had already been in the tomb for four days. Bethany was less than two miles from Jerusalem, and many Jews had come to Martha and Mary to comfort them in the loss of their brother. When Martha heard that Jesus was coming, she went out to meet him, but Mary stayed at home.

"Lord," Martha said to Jesus, "if you had been here, my brother would not have died. But I know that even now God will give you whatever you ask."

Jesus said to her, "Your brother will rise again."

Martha answered, "I know he will rise again in the resurrection at the last day."

Jesus said to her, "I am the resurrection and the life. He who believes in me will live, even though he dies; and whoever lives and believes in me will never die. Do you believe this?"

"Yes, Lord," she told him, "I believe that you are the Christ, the Son of God, who was to come into the world."

When Mary reached the place where Jesus was and saw him, she fell at his feet and said, "Lord, if you had been here, my brother would not have died."

When Jesus saw her weeping, and the Jews who had come along with her also weeping, he was deeply moved in spirit and troubled. "Where have you laid him?" he asked.

"Come and see, Lord," they replied.

Jesus wept.

Then the Jews said, "See how he loved him!"

But some of them said, "Could not he who opened the eyes of the blind man have kept this man from dying?"

Jesus, once more deeply moved, came to the tomb. It was a cave with a stone laid across the entrance. "Take away the stone," he said.

"But, Lord," said Martha, the sister of the dead man, "by this time there is a bad odor, for he has been there four days."

Daughter of Confidence

Then Jesus said, "Did I not tell you that if you believed, you would see the glory of God?"

So they took away the stone. Then Jesus looked up and said, "Father, I thank you that you have heard me. I knew that you always hear me, but I said this for the benefit of the people standing here, that they may believe that you sent me."

When he had said this, Jesus called in a loud voice, "Lazarus, come out!" The dead man came out, his hands and feet wrapped with strips of linen, and a cloth around his face.

Jesus said to them, "Take off the grave clothes and let him go."

—John 11:17–27, 32–44

Reflections on how my faith has grown through hard times…

_____

_____

_____

_____

_____

_____

_____

_____

_____

_____

_____

_____

For you have been my hope, O Sovereign LORD,
my confidence since my youth.
—Psalm 71:5

_In him and through faith in him we may approach God
with freedom and confidence._
—Ephesians 3:12

_Let us then approach the throne of grace with confidence,
so that we may receive mercy and find grace to help us
in our time of need. — Hebrews 4:16_

Chapter 5

Daughter of Boldness

Stand firm in your faith as a woman of courage. I haven't given you a spirit of timidity, but a spirit of power, of love, and of self-discipline. Through faith in Jesus, you can approach Me with freedom and confidence. Remember, you can do all things through Christ who strengthens you. I fortify you with My own great power, so you can demonstrate boldness even standing alone.

Love,
The Lord
Your Rock

—from 1 Corinthians 16:13; 2 Timothy 1:7;

Ephesians 3:12; Philippians 4:13; Colossians 1:10–11

As a woman, how do you see your role in society? In the church? In your own family? Throughout most of history, a woman's role has been dictated in one way or another by men. Some good men. Some not-so-good men. But there comes a time when the only decree that matters is God's. There comes a time when you, as a woman, must stand alone, face to face, toe to toe, heart to heart with God and give an answer for who you are—not who others think you should be.

So, who are you? Why were you created? What is your purpose? What should you be doing with your life? Why are you here? Tough questions and ones that fortunately or unfortunately (depending on your perspective) take a lifetime to answer. So you'd better get started!

Of course there will be those who will want to help you with the answers—tell you what you can and cannot do, tell you what your boundaries are or are not. But the trick is to enter the room of life, seek and find Jesus, and then never take your eyes off of Him—no matter how loud the clamoring around you gets!

But how do you go about it all? How do you know you're doing the right thing?

Answer: You remember Whose you are! You bow

your head, ask for guidance, and then bravely walk across the room toward Jesus.

Every day you petition for the boldness of the apostle Peter—the boldness that empowered him to climb out of that boat onto the icy waters about him. You pray for the submissive and faithful heart of Mary when the angel Gabriel told her of her destiny. And finally, but most importantly, you humble yourself each day as Christ humbled Himself on the cross—when those around Him still did not believe.

That's how.

Woman was God's idea. Make Him proud.

We do not strive for spectacular actions.

What counts is the gift of yourself, the degree

of love you put into each of your deeds.

—MOTHER TERESA

 Make Him Proud

She slipped into the crowded room unnoticed. Her heart thundered in her chest. As each beat grew louder, she wondered how those in the room could not hear it. It was as though a storm was raging inside of her, crashing and thrashing in icy waves over her heart. The momentum of its power caught her in a whirlpool—tossing her mind, heart, and soul until they were battered, bruised, and exhausted.

If she could just catch His eye, she would know!

Through the parted shoulders of the men in front of her, she caught a glimpse of Him reclining at the table at the seat of honor. His forearm and a quick sliver of His face were all that she could see as she slowly moved along the fence of humanity that pressed in on Him. Men of reputation, intelligence, faith, and power stood between her and Him. With one glance they could banish her from the room. For what she was about to do, they could even order her killed. At that thought, she had to force herself to try to breathe normally.

How beautiful He was! Her eyes never left where He was sitting, as she maneuvered her way ever so slowly around the sea of men. Her movements became as a dance—fluid, graceful, silent. A hand, a lock of hair, a tanned foot—she was close enough now to catch snippets of His words. *His voice must be what heaven sounds like,* she thought.

Finally she was only five steps from Him. Five steps—yet hundreds of years of tradition and law separated them.

Her eyes never left His face. If she were to do this, she must not look away. Her only source of courage could be found in His gaze and His face alone.

If He would just look at her, she would know!

And then, as if He heard the pleading of her heart, His

eyes embraced her. Enveloped her. Invaded every part of her...

...and the storm stopped.

One step. Her knees almost buckled.

Two steps. She could no longer breathe.

Three steps. The room fell silent.

Four steps. She could not stop the tears.

Five steps. The joy! The joy!

She knelt down and took the small bottle of fragrant oil from around her neck as she gently placed the feet of her love—her Savior—on her lap. Her tears blurred the room. At first her hands shook, making it impossible for her to remove the dainty cork out of the miniature jar. He reached out and took her hands in His. The tremors immediately obeyed His touch. With steady hands and a calm heart, she now bravely continued her humble offering.

She was created for this moment—of this she had no doubt. With His eyes upon her, her hands performed the sacrament of love without hesitation. The oil flowed as a stream over His ankles and heels and between His toes.

The room of men sat dumbfounded. What was happening? All eyes turned to Jesus—questioning, gawking, judging, yearning, hoping, trusting, distrusting. Hardened hearts would not allow understanding. What the Son and the Father had set in motion centuries before was only days from coming to pass, yet most in the room were oblivious. The Messiah was sharing His final hours with them, yet what consumed them was their own self-interest and their precious decorum. All that mattered to them was that this woman was committing an abominable act. Voices were found. Anger exploded. Ridicule ruled.

"Stop her!" "She's a sinner!" "She wastes precious resources!"

As for the woman, she no longer heard the rattle of the chains that for centuries kept "her kind" in place. She smiled up at Jesus. The love that was reflected in His eyes fortified her courage, redeemed her boldness, and placed in her soul acceptance, worth, and mission.

"Be silent," said the Savior. "She prepares me for my Father."

Make Him Proud

The muttering did not completely cease. Hearts were blackened. Yet this woman—this seemingly incidental woman—did what no man in that room would: She defied her tradition and walked boldly toward God.

The woman finished her ceremony by drying His feet with her cascading hair. They stood as one, and she knew that life as it had been no longer existed. She was now accountable to her Savior. Her existence was validated. Her purpose was clear. She turned and walked back across the room—never to be afraid again.

Scriptural Account

While he was in Bethany, reclining at the table in the home of a man known as Simon the Leper, a woman came with an alabaster jar of very expensive perfume, made of pure nard. She broke the jar and poured the perfume on his head.

Some of those present were saying indignantly to one another, "Why this waste of perfume? It could have been sold for more than a year's wages and the money given to the poor." And they rebuked her harshly.

Daughter of Boldness

"Leave her alone," said Jesus. "Why are you bothering her? She has done a beautiful thing to me. The poor you will always have with you, and you can help them any time you want. But you will not always have me. She did what she could. She poured perfume on my body beforehand to prepare for my burial. I tell you the truth, wherever the gospel is preached throughout the world, what she has done will also be told, in memory of her."

—Mark 14:3–9

Reflections on times I have taken a bold step of faith…

_____

_____

_____

_____

_____

_____

_____

_____

_____

_____

_____

_____

_____

When I called, you answered me;
you made me bold and stouthearted.
—Psalm 138:3

_____

_____

_____

_____

_____

_____

_____

_____

_____

_____

_____

_____

_____

_____

Therefore, since we have such a hope, we are very bold.
—2 Corinthians 3:12

_____

_____

_____

_____

_____

_____

_____

_____

_____

_____

_____

_____

But Christ is faithful as a son over God's house.
And we are his house, if we hold on to our courage
and the hope of which we boast. —Hebrews 3:6

Chapter 6

Daughter of Determination

Even tiny faith has mountain-moving potential. Make the most of every opportunity. Rid yourself of entangling sin and everything that holds you back from being the woman of faith I've created you to be. May you run with endurance the race of life I've already marked out for you, fixing your eyes upon Me.

Love,
The Author and Perfector of Your Faith

—from Matthew 17:20; Colossians 4:5; Hebrews 12:1–2

Have you ever shrunk from an opportunity out of fear? Kept silent out of self-doubt? Squelched laughter out of self-consciousness?

When you do that, do you realize that you are guilty of replacing that ancient veil of restriction over your face? That you are shackling yourself with a chain that was forged out of anxiety and apprehension?

It's true. How many times have you missed opportunities to demonstrate God's glory because you lacked boldness? For example: It is common knowledge that your boss, who is aloof to everyone, is experiencing a personal trauma—dare you let her know that you're praying for her? The water-cooler bunch is ridiculing yet another coworker—what do you do? Your friend is heading down a path that could destroy her marriage—do you keep silent? The joke was on you; it was harmless, it was fun—can you laugh at yourself or not?

God wants you to stand up straight, look the world in the eye, and proclaim Him God, Father of all. On that sixth day of creation, something wonderful happened: God decided that man needed a partner—so here you are!

He made you strong. He gave you your voice. He expects great things.

What if Queen Esther had not stood up to the wicked Haaman?

What if Noah's wife had been too afraid to enter the ark?

What if Jocobed had not placed her infant son, Moses, into the basket?

And can you imagine…what if Mary had said no to Gabriel?

Talk about missed opportunities!

If you step forward, He'll push the demons back.

If you stand for good, He'll bridle the evil.

If you proclaim the cross, He'll teach you the victory dance.

Fear not! Go boldly.

Announce the King!

Faith means believing in advance what

will only make sense in reverse.

—PHILIP YANCEY

Fear Not!

She had paced the borders of Tyre and Sidon for hours—waiting, watching. At times, she would sit and rest on the banks of the Great Sea and allow the lapping of the water upon the shore to calm her spirit. Other times she would simply stand still and strain her eyes, looking into the distance, hoping to see Him emerge across the plain.

"He must come soon," she'd mutter to herself—she felt her daughter would not last much longer. The Jewish Healer was rumored to be coming this way. Why He was daring to cross into enemy territory was beyond her. But if He didn't come soon, she swore she would cross the boundaries into

Palestine herself to find Him. Her daughter was near death and madness—held captive by Satan. Her only hope was in the one they called the Son of David. The stories she had heard of His miraculous powers quickened her heart. For the sake of her daughter, nothing would keep her from Him.

The Gentile woman was stricken with desperation, but her heart was as strong as cedar. She was determined not to leave the Healer alone until He slew whatever evil dangled her daughter over a flame. She would not allow Him to turn her away. She would not fail to seize this opportunity.

And then she saw them. The man, Jesus, and His followers appeared on the horizon. Immediately she began running after them and shouting, "Have mercy on me, O Lord, Son of David; my daughter is cruelly demon-possessed!"

Expecting to see a half-crazed woman crawling toward them, all the men turned to look at her. Instead, what they saw was a woman convicted, committed, and kicking up dust in her stride.

Her clothing told them instantly of her Gentile heritage. Her rapid march toward them signified her determination. Some of the men in the crowd made fun of the trailing woman. Others were displeased at her presence and were hopeful she would get discouraged and turn back. But Jesus could hear her steps quickening and feel the beckoning of her pain. He admired her courage, and His heart was pulled toward her.

The cross was crooning Jesus' name louder and louder. Time was short, yet this woman's determination granted Him reprieve through her faith and courage. She knew who He was! Her boldness reminded Him that the message of His mission would not be lost in the fateful days to come.

Jesus continued walking and gave the pretense of ignoring the woman. But the woman would not be deterred. "He *will* stop and listen to me, even if I have to follow Him to Jerusalem and back!" she vowed.

The woman continued her desperate cries as she ran beside the Healer. At one point she thought she saw Him almost smile and look at her out of the corner of His eye. This encouraged her and made her think that maybe Jesus was not as annoyed with her as she first thought. Hopeful of this, she continued her pleading as she walked along beside Him. Even though He did not seem annoyed, His friends did. "Do what she wants and then send her away!" they pleaded with Jesus.

Without missing a step, Jesus maneuvered around the stones in the path and spoke to the men words she knew were meant for her: "I was sent only to the lost sheep of the house of Israel."

But I am lost, and my daughter is hopelessly lost. You, Son of David, Son of God, are our only salvation! shouted the voice in her heart. Seizing the moment and not knowing what else to do, she ran before Him and fell at His feet. "Lord, help me!" she pleaded.

An eternity crept by as the woman lay her forehead on the feet of Jesus. She dared not look up. The comfort of touching even the slightest part of Him cooled the searing in her skull.

Then she heard His voice speak directly into her open heart: "It is not good to take the children's bread and throw it to the pet dog."

This was it—the only opportunity she may have to save her daughter. With a boldness she could not explain and a fearlessness she had never experienced, she looked Jesus directly in the eye and said, "Yes, Lord; but even the pet dog feeds on the crumbs which fall from its master's table."

The Creator of this woman smiled at her with pride and said, "Dear woman, your faith is great; be it done for you as you wish."

The Canaanite woman could not take her eyes off Jesus. She memorized the crook of His smile, the arch of His eyebrows, and the smudge of sweat on His forehead. The hot sun haloed His form, and His shadow shaded her soul. The strangling fist that held her heart at its mercy loosened its grip. Her daughter was freed at this moment—of that she had no doubt. And this woman—this bold, determined woman—bowed to her King.

Scriptural Account

A Canaanite woman from that vicinity came to him, crying out, "Lord, Son of David, have mercy on me! My daughter is suffering terribly from demon-possession."

Jesus did not answer a word. So his disciples came to him and urged him, "Send her away, for she keeps crying out after us."

Daughter of Determination

He answered, "I was sent only to the lost sheep of Israel."

The woman came and knelt before him. "Lord, help me!" she said.

He replied, "It is not right to take the children's bread and toss it to their dogs."

"Yes, Lord," she said, "but even the dogs eat the crumbs that fall from their masters' table."

Then Jesus answered, "Woman, you have great faith! Your request is granted." And her daughter was healed from that very hour.

—Matthew 15:22–28

Reflections on times I have overcome my fears
with God's help…

_____

_____

_____

_____

_____

_____

_____

_____

_____

_____

_____

_____

_____

But I trust in your unfailing love;
my heart rejoices in your salvation.
—Psalm 13:5

_____

_____

_____

_____

_____

_____

_____

_____

_____

_____

_____

_____

_____

Those who know your name will trust in you, for you, LORD,
have never forsaken those who seek you.
—Psalm 9:10

Let the morning bring me word of your unfailing love,
for I have put my trust in you.
—Psalm 143:8

Chapter 7

Daughter of Trust

When you give, My blessings will boomerang back to you—pressed down, shaken together, and overflowing. Test Me and see if I won't throw open the floodgates of heaven, pouring out so much blessing that you can't contain it. May you feast on My abundance and drink from My river of delight. I'm more than able to provide all of your needs according to My unlimited riches in glory.

Generously,

Your Trustworthy God

—from Luke 6:38; Malachi 3:10; Psalm 36:8; Philippians 4:19

God will take care of you. He will!

However…faith, like love, usually comes with a price. Letting go of the handrail. Taking off the training wheels. Stepping away from the ledge. It's scary, wobbly, and makes your heart pound in your ears. But once you've done it, there's no turning back—not because you can't, but because you don't want to.

Once you've experienced what it's like to allow God to release His power in your life, it's hard to settle for anything less. Faith means doing the unexpected while the world rolls its eyes.

Are you unsure of your next step? Confused about your future? Afraid of what's around the bend? Have you ever considered that's just the way God wants you? Sometimes, He does His best work when you don't have a clue. At times like these, all you need to know is that He does!

God is in the details. Not your details—*His* details. Sparrows don't plan for the future, yet they return in the spring year after year, fat and sassy. Lilies don't grow tall and beautiful because they know how, but because God does.

So if God has time to tend to birds and flowers, don't you think you are on His agenda someplace? After all, you're family.

Don't look back. Leap. And pray while you run!

Our faith comes in moments…

yet there is a depth in those brief

moments which constrains us to ascribe more

reality to them than to all other experiences.

—RALPH WALDO EMERSON

God Is Good

As the widow descended the steps of the Beautiful Gate, her meager leather sandals clattered upon the marble courtyard. The magnificence of the Temple surrounding her made her goat-hair mourning cloak seem even more drab and harsh. Her skin crawled and itched from its coarseness. Its smell caused her stomach to wretch. Yet she wore her widow's garb with straight shoulders. Her life with her husband had been good, even though she had no child to prove it. They had been happy—just the two of them. Blessed. She made the baskets. He sold them at market. At night she would sit as his feet, and he would stroke her hair.

Daughter of Trust

God had been good.

The chatter around her grew louder as she walked to the center of the Court of Women. All along the colonnades people were in line, waiting to drop their offering into a treasury chest. The time of sacrifice had passed for the day. For the remaining worshipers, thirteen chests lined the courtyard wall for the convenience of a personal offering.

As she chose her position in line, she kept her head down. Veiled. Covered. Cloaked in modesty. Her hands were hidden by the length of her sleeves. In her cupped palm was the last of her allowance—two copper coins given to her by her late husband's brother. He was now her master. He chose not to marry her, but allowed her to work as a slave and to sleep in a closet in the back of his house—the house that was once hers. She didn't know if she would receive another allowance. Her lamp needed oil, and her share of the pantry grain was almost gone. With that thought her stomach became unruly and growled. But she would not think of that now. She had come here to give back—not to ask for more.

God had been good.

It never ceased to amaze her how close to His presence she

felt here. It was only in this place that the burden of loneliness did not overpower her. When she passed through Solomon's Porch and entered the Beautiful Gate, the fog over her heart lifted. This holy place buoyed her spirit and convinced her that it would be *all right*—all of it: the empty jar of oil, the bare grain cupboard, her barren womb, her husbandless nights. Here, she was able to will her panic away.

As she stepped closer to the treasury, the coins shifted in her hand. How small they were. *If only I had more to give,* her heart sighed.

Through her veil, she could see the finery of those before her. They gave their gold and silver with big gestures. How miserable her copper coins would look among the abundance and glitter.

"Father, forgive me, for this is all I have," she prayed. With her eyes downward, her posture submissive, the widow brought the tiny coins to her lips, kissed them, and then gently dropped them through the trumpet-like receptacle.

Jesus and His disciples had been sitting on the steps of Nicanor Gate, observing the crowd in the Court of Women. He watched as an endless line of people dropped their coins into the treasury. The showmanship of the wealthy as they approached the treasury reminded Jesus of court jesters. How silly they looked, strutting and squawking as they deposited their large coins. The purpose of their gift was totally lost among the fanfare.

Suddenly Jesus' eyes became riveted upon a solitary figure. Out of the hundreds before Him, it was her heart alone that cried out to Him. The strength of the widow's faith became a balm to soothe the abrasive day. Its purity beckoned angels to gather about the court simply to be in her presence.

Jesus got up and climbed several more steps so He could see her better. Those in the Holy Realms held their breath as she stepped forward to take her turn at the treasury. Out of her mourning, she undauntedly celebrated His power. Out of her poverty, she outgave the richest of men!

As her veil, worn from years of use, pulled at its seams, she kept her eyes downward. It pained Jesus to know what her gift cost her. He knew that tonight she would go to bed hungry. He knew on this night she would sit alone in the dark and wait for dawn.

God Is Good

Everything about her conflicted Jesus' heart. Her poverty and circumstances jabbed at Him like poisonous spears. Yet her faith and unselfishness filled Him up like fresh morning air. And then there was the spectacle before Him of the foolish ones—plump and spoiled, tossing in their gold coins like worthless seeds. They acted as if they were buying a place in His throne room with their silly crumbs. To His followers, Jesus said, "Truly, that widow put in more than all of them!"

As it turned out that night, the woman had no need for a lamp or oil. Miraculously her tiny room was as light as day, as if the moon sat over her doorpost and the stars danced in the corners. She slept—not wrestling with hunger, but with the luscious feeling of fullness and contentment. Outside an angel stood guard with his orders: Her sleep was not to be disturbed, jasmine was to fill the air around her, and her dreams were to be very, very sweet.

God is good.

Scriptural Account

Jesus sat down opposite the place where the offerings were put and watched the crowd putting their money into the temple treasury. Many rich people threw in large amounts. But a poor widow came and put in two very small copper coins, worth only a fraction of a penny.

Calling his disciples to him, Jesus said, "I tell you the truth, this poor widow has put more into the treasury than all the others. They all gave out of their wealth; but she, out of her poverty, put in everything—all she had to live on."

—Mark 12:41–44

Reflections on how God has taken care of me...

_____

_____

_____

_____

_____

_____

_____

_____

_____

_____

_____

_____

_____

We will not fear, though the earth give way
and the mountains fall into the heart of the sea.
—Psalm 46:2

*A generous man will prosper;
he who refreshes others will himself be refreshed.*
—*Proverbs 11:25*

_____

_____

_____

_____

_____

_____

_____

_____

_____

_____

_____

Give, and it will be given to you. A good measure, pressed down,
shaken together and running over, will be poured into your lap.
For with the measure you use, it will be measured to you.
—Luke 6:38

The giant step in the walk of faith is the one
we take when we decide God no longer is a
part of our lives. He is our life.

—BETH MOORE